All About
SHARKS

Units of Measure

John Lockyer

Publishing Credits

Editor
Sara Johnson

Editorial Director
Emily R. Smith, M.A.Ed.

Editor-in-Chief
Sharon Coan, M.S.Ed.

Creative Director
Lee Aucoin

Publisher
Rachelle Cracchiolo, M.S.Ed.

Image Credits

Teacher Created Materials

5301 Oceanus Drive
Huntington Beach, CA 92649-1030
http://www.tcmpub.com
ISBN 978-0-7439-0904-4
© 2009 Teacher Created Materials, Inc.
Reprinted 2013

Table of Contents

Sharks

When you think about the ocean, what animals do you think of? Perhaps you think of fish. If you do, then you could be thinking about sharks. Sharks are fish.

There are about 350 different **species** (SPEE-seez) of sharks in the world.

Slow Swimmer

The wobbegong (WOB-ee-gong) shark swims slowly along the seabed. Its speed is less than 0.6 miles per hour (1 km/h).

Fast Swimmer

This mako shark swims so fast, it can jump right out of the water. It reaches speeds of 19 miles per hour (30 km/h) and can leap nearly 20 feet (6 m) in the air.

LET'S EXPLORE MATH

Inches and feet are **units** of measurement. They measure length. The mako shark can leap up to 20 feet in the air.

a. About how many inches is this?
Hint: 12 inches = 1 foot

The mako shark can swim at a speed of 19 miles per hour.

b. If the shark swam a distance of 76 miles, how many hours was it swimming?

Bodies Without Bones

Unlike many other fish, sharks do not have bones. They have **skeletons** (SKEL-uh-tuhns) made of **cartilage** (CAR-tuh-lij). You have cartilage in your ears and your nose.

A shark's body shape helps it swim well through water. Its strong fins move it forward.

gills

head

snout

Sharks have **gills**, which they use to breathe under water. Sharks have 5 to 7 rows of gills.

dorsal fin

tail fin

fins

Smallest Shark
The smallest shark is the dwarf dogfish. It grows to about 6 inches (15 cm) and weighs just 1.5 ounces (42 g). It is small enough to fit into an adult's hand.

Ancient Sharks

Different sharks have lived in the ocean for almost 400 million years. The megalodon (MEG-uh-luh-don) shark lived 1.6 to 16 million years ago.

megalodon shark

A megalodon shark tooth

The megalodon measured up to 50 feet (15 m) in length. Its jaws were 6.5 feet (2 m) wide. Its teeth were up to 8 inches (20 cm) long. It weighed around 20 tons (18,144 kg), which is as much as 5 elephants.

A megalodon shark was around 3 times the length of a great white shark.

great white shark

LET'S EXPLORE MATH

A ton is used to measure large amounts of weight. A megalodon could weigh as much as 5 elephants, or a total of 20 tons.

a. About how much does each elephant weigh?

Megalodon teeth were up to 20 centimeters in length. Great white shark teeth are around 5 centimeters in length.

b. How many times bigger is the megalodon tooth?

Heads and Tails

Today, more than half of all shark species are less than 3 feet (1 m) long. But some species grow much larger and have unusual features.

The hammerhead shark has eyes on the ends of its head. It swings its head from side to side to see. Its head can grow up to half as long as its body.

The hammerhead shark measures around 12 feet (up to 4 m) in length. Yet it can be found swimming in water less than 3 feet (1 m) deep.

Thresher sharks use their tails to slap and slash other fish. This makes their **prey** easier to catch and eat. Their tails can grow as long as their bodies.

A thresher shark can grow up to 15 feet (5 m) long.

Teeth

Sharks often lose their teeth when they are catching their prey. So they are always growing new teeth. Sharks can have up to 3,000 teeth at a time. Shark teeth often grow in rows of 5. A shark can go through 30,000 teeth in a lifetime!

LET'S EXPLORE MATH

Pounds (lbs.) and ounces (oz.) are used to measure amounts of weight. *Hint:* 1 pound = 16 ounces

a. A great white shark can eat 20 pounds in 1 mouthful. How many ounces is that?

b. How many ounces are there in ½ a pound?

Great Teeth

Great white sharks have sharp, jagged teeth for biting and tearing. They can take 20 pounds (9 kg) out of their prey in each bite!

Dorsal Fins

The fin on top of a shark's back is called the dorsal fin. It is this fin that can often be seen above the water. Dorsal fins are stiff. A shark's fins help it stay upright in the water. All sharks have 1 or 2 dorsal fins.

Dorsal Fins

Shark	Height of Dorsal Fin
dwarf dogfish	2.5 cm
cookie-cutter shark	3.75 cm
angel shark	10 cm
bullhead shark	20 cm
thresher shark	33 cm
Greenland shark	50 cm
basking shark	100 cm
great white shark	100 cm
whale shark	228 cm

dorsal fin

LET'S EXPLORE MATH

Centimeters can also be used to measure length.
Use the table on page 14 to answer these questions.
Hint: 10 millimeters = 1 centimeter

a. How many millimeters is the dorsal fin of an angel shark?

b. Which shark(s) has a dorsal fin(s) measuring 1,000 millimeters in length?

c. The length of a bullhead shark's dorsal fin is:

    1. 2 millimeters **2.** 20 millimeters **3.** 200 millimeters

Which Oceans?

Sharks are found in all the world's oceans. They live in many different ocean depths. But most sharks live in warm, sunlit waters to depths of 650 feet (200 m). The water temperature here is 50°F to 68°F (10°C to 20°C).

Seabed Swimmers

Angel sharks live on the seabed, near coastlines, where the water temperature is above 68°F (20°C).

A white-tipped reef shark hunts for food in the warm, sunlit water above a coral reef.

Whale Sharks

The whale shark is the biggest fish in the world. It grows more than 40 feet (12 m) long and can weigh up to 13 tons (11,793 kg). Whale sharks are slow swimmers. They have a top speed of 3 miles per hour (5 km/h).

A whale shark is about the length of a school bus.

Big Mouth!

Whale sharks swim with their mouths open. They suck in water that is filled with **plankton** (PLANK-tuhn) and small fish. Whale sharks' mouths can be 5 feet (1.5 m) wide. They can suck in over 1,500 gallons (6,000 L) of water an hour.

LET'S EXPLORE MATH

Liters and milliliters are used to measure amounts of liquid. A whale shark can suck in 6,000 liters of water in an hour.

Hint: 1 liter = 1,000 milliliters

a. How many milliliters are there in 6 liters?

b. How many milliliters are there in 1 ½ liters?

Great White Sharks

Great white sharks are one of the most famous species of shark. Movies have even been made about them! Most great white sharks grow to between 12 and 20 feet (about 3.5 to 6 m) long. That's about as long as a van.

Fast Movers

Great white sharks are amazing hunters. They can reach speeds of 25 miles per hour (40 km/h) and can leap out of the water to catch their prey.

LET'S EXPLORE MATH

Which of these units of measurement do you think best describes the weight of a great white shark? Write at least 2 sentences explaining your answer.

a. 20 kilograms

c. 2 tons

b. 2 pounds

d. 20 pounds

Strange Sharks

The swell shark sucks water in when it gets scared. It can blow itself up to 3 times its normal size. It can wedge itself between rocks. That means no **predator** (PRED-uh-ter) can get it out.

swell shark

This cookie-cutter shark has long, sharp teeth. It bites and holds onto bigger prey. When it lets go, the bite looks like a cookie shape.

This dolphin has been bitten by a cookie-cutter shark.

Under Attack?

Some people think sharks are very dangerous animals. But only 50 to 75 shark attacks are reported each year. Yet around 100 million sharks are caught and killed each year.

A shark caught in a fishing net

Sharks are killed for their meat. Parts of sharks are also used in clothes and lotions. Many sharks are trapped in fishing nets and die. Scientists are worried that sharks are being killed before they have babies. This means there will be fewer sharks in the future.

Shark Babies

Shark babies are called pups. A great white shark pup is about 4 feet (1.2 m) long when it is born and weighs around 40 pounds (18 kg). That is about the same size you were when you were 5 years old!

shark pup

Studying Sharks

Scientists want to learn more about sharks. They do this in different ways. Some climb into cages and go in the water to film the sharks. Other scientists swim with sharks. They have to wear special diving suits to keep safe! These people help us learn more about these amazing fish.

Shark Measurements

Shark	Average length	Average weight
dwarf dogfish	6 inches (15 cm)	1.5 ounces (43 g)
cookie-cutter shark	20 inches (50 cm)	5.5 ounces (156 g)
bullhead shark	40 inches (1 m)	20 pounds (9 kg)
angel shark	5 feet (1.5 m)	66 pounds (30 kg)
thresher shark	15 feet (4.5 m)	350 pounds (159 kg)
Greenland shark	20 feet (6 m)	2,200 pounds (998 kg)
great white shark	20 feet (6 m)	7,000 pounds (3,200 kg)
basking shark	33 feet (10 m)	15,400 pounds (6,985 kg)
whale shark	40 feet (12 m)	28,700 pounds (13,018 kg)

Use the table above to answer these questions.

a. Which shark measures exactly 5 yards in length?
Hint: 1 yard = 3 feet.

b. Which shark is exactly twice the length of the cookie-cutter shark?

c. How many bullhead sharks make up a total weight of 100 pounds?

Sharks in the Classroom

Students at Seaview Elementary have been learning about sharks. They want to make life-size shark pictures to display on their classroom walls. Each wall of the classroom is 45 feet (13.7 m) in length.

The students decide to display pictures of the following sharks:

Type of Shark	Length of Shark
thresher	15 feet (4.5 m)
angel	5 feet (1.5 m)
Greenland	20 feet (6 m)
bullhead	3 feet (0.9 m)

Solve It!

Use the information in the table to answer the questions below. Note that the pictures will be displayed end to end.

a. How many thresher shark pictures can fit on 1 wall?

b. How many angel shark pictures can fit on 1 wall?

c. How many Greenland shark pictures can fit on 1 wall?

d. How many bullhead shark pictures can fit on 1 wall?

e. Explain how you solved questions **a** and **d**.

Glossary

cartilage—firm elastic tissue in the body

gills—organs in fish that take oxygen from the water

plankton—very tiny plants and animals that float in water

predator—hunter

prey—an animal that is hunted and killed by another animal for food

skeletons—the bones of an animal

species—kinds of animals

units—measurements of quantity

Index

Let's Explore Math

Page 5:
a. 1 foot = 12 inches, so 20 feet × 12 inches = 240 inches
b. 76 miles ÷ 19 miles per hour = 4 hours

Page 9:
a. 20 tons ÷ 5 elephants = 4 tons each
b. 20 cm ÷ 5 cm = 4 times bigger

Page 12:
a. 20 × 16 = 320 ounces   **b.** 16 ounces ÷ 2 = 8 ounces

Page 15:
a. 100 millimeters
b. The basking shark and the great white shark
c. 3. 200 millimeters in length

Page 19:
a. 6 × 1,000 = 6,000 milliliters
b. 1 liter = 1,000 milliliters; ½ liter = 500 milliliters
  1,000 + 500 = 1,500 milliliters

Page 21:
c. 2 tons
Explanations will vary.

Page 27:
a. The thresher shark
b. The bullhead shark
c. 5 bullhead sharks

Problem-Solving Activity

a. A thresher shark is 15 feet in length. 15 feet × 3 = 45 feet, so 3 thresher shark pictures can fit on 1 wall.

b. 45 feet ÷ 5 feet = 9 feet, so 9 angel shark pictures can fit on 1 wall.

c. 20 feet + 20 feet = 40 feet. Only 2 full-size Greenland shark pictures can fit on a 45-foot wall.

d. A bullhead shark is 3 feet in length. 45 feet ÷ 3 feet = 15 feet, so 15 bullhead shark pictures can fit on 1 wall.

e. Answers will vary.